Repeat Slowly, Like Dance

Poems by Cheryl Vargas

Iniquity Press/Vendetta Books
Published by Dave Roskos
PO Box 253 • Seaside Heights NJ 08751

Cover Art: *Night-light* by Hannah Vargas
16in x 12in mixed media on canvas

Photographer: Eleanor Jean

Design & layout: Angela Mark

for my brother, Harry Brandt III

Table of Contents

1. The Ladies Of Schwin Drive
2. Solitude
3. Muslin Now
4. Song Sung Blue, Overlook Hospital, Summit NJ
5. Iris
6. Off My Mark
7. Flecks Of Light
8. Cucina Povera
9. A Distorted Image
10. Aubade In The Afternoon
11. Forty Weeks Times Six
12. Nameless Bakery
13. A Bit On The Side
14. Kaleidoscope Vision
15. Borrowed And Blue
16. Hothouse
17. Pillow Talk
18. The Phone Never Rang This Morning
19. Roadside Memorial, Route 80, (To Michigan)
20. Homestead Farm At Oak Ridge
21. Effervescent Memories
22. Abundance
23. Moving On

The Ladies Of Schwin Drive

My mother never wasted time baking cookies; she played poker instead. No additional time spent deciphering exact measurements—after all, Italian women don't measure ingredients. *Store-bought cookies are just fine.* The vessel that held the subpar cookies allowed her freedom from the stove. It was filled exclusively with our 16th president's profile, no poker chips. I can still hear the jingle of the copper penny wind chime. Once a month, four additional non-bakers emerged from their 1960s cookie-cutter homes, Jell-O molds in hand. A game of chance, no husbands allowed. From my bed, I could hear the sound of carefree women. To this day, I still can't figure if two of a kind beats a full house. I am more of a solitaire woman.

Solitude

She rests beneath a cascade of flowers like Ophelia in that pre-Raphaelite painting. The earth yawns. A sky awakens. Clouds make their own waves over turquoise sea. She fashions an Irish lace shawl. The tree's knotty trunk is as strong as her lover's arms and she leans as lovers do. Twigs coated in mud artisan-style house unborn robbins. The nest hidden on a short branch, distributes the weight. She carries hers daily in her shoulders. Birds whisper and she listens. Their secrets safe with her. Carries fragrant blooms that remain on her dress, as well as his scent. Her beloved Cherry Blossom tree absorbs it all. A Japanese parasol protects her identity.

Muslin Now

1.

I ask you to lean against me, allow the weight to shift, as I lower your body onto the shower stool. The curtain creates a puddle of water upon the blush pink tile floor, a lipstick color favored years ago. I wash your muslin skin as I recall the pale forsythia bloomed outside the bathroom window. I wrap a towel around you. The softness creates a safe space between us.

2.

Another day. Slivers of light dance over your body. A sunrise on the lake. Change, wash, brush teeth, comb hair, a dab of perfume, why not?

Elevate the conversation, your legs too. The oxygen tank hums. I turn up Frank Sinatra on the old record player to croon over the hideous noise.

3.

The hospital bed takes up space in my childhood bedroom. Death announces itself. You sleep between thin sheets. Your silhouette's reflection in a portrait of a young woman, in a white gown with satin buttons. Our sterile conversations fill the spare space. Dad, a room away, alone. Death leans in, listens.

Song Sung Blue, Overlook Hospital Summit, New Jersey

When I look at the scar on my knee I see the shadow of a lovely boy. The nurse who changed my dressing seemed pleased. Black thread sewn below my kneecap, a visual tattoo that my skin was the fabric of my body. A routine surgery, ten days, and I would be back to practicing my dance moves for prom. The tight black stitches tore away from the skin. Gangrene was a term I heard in Civil War movies. Neil said he'd still like me with a wooden leg. The nurses let us share our dinners together. Neil gave me his jello. There was a second surgery and weeks bound to a hospital bed. We danced without the dance.

Iris

Roots planted deep,
the equinox held promise.

Pushed hard to break ground she abandons
her cold bed. A new bloom.

Off My Mark

Smack on the lips! The kiss on the cheek went awry. Overshot my target three inches left. Landed on his mouth. It all happened so quickly. I followed through. Although completed with a subpar version of my best work, like some knockoff Gustav Klimt. The train slipped the track. Why didn't I just do it properly? After all, I was already in the perfect spot. Take my time like lovers do, lean in, hold his face, a hand on each cheek feel his beard, young thorns on a dining car rose. Guide his out of focus gaze, his soft eyes, a hazy silhouette. Embrace him, steal his breath, bite his lower lip. Repeat slowly, like dance. Spend a lifetime. Softly pull back a slow sunset beneath the horizon. A butterfly whisper across his lips, then finish on the exhale, my wind chimes to his train whistle. Bring him back into focus. Allow him to return the gesture. His locomotive kiss. *Smack* his cheek!

Flecks Of Light

He gazes at me as I spy his shadow dancing upon the water. Soft as a breeze, I whisper to him. *Swim with me. Swim alongside me for I will not lead, dive deep down hold your breath, hold me.* Beneath the surface darkness will protect us. No voices filling our heads. A mermaid of dream.

Cucina Povera

We built the chicken coup last spring simple and strong, and gave each hen a proper name. Eight, still warm, tan-speckled eggs nestle in my wicker basket. Your pale freckles rest upon the bridge of your nose. These delicate wonders are the foundation to our frittata. A meal that satisfies desires that run deep. You give the crisp vegetables a rough chop. I lean in close, mindful of the sharp blade. The cast iron skillet patiently waits, seasoned and reliable like my grandparents' marriage with Neapolitan roots thick as the olive oil that coats the frying pan. "Friggere" creates translucent veggies, a softness that lingers upon scarlet lips, a roosters' wattle. Combined with salty cheese, a rustic pairing and humble cuisine. Bake at a high temperature, the edges crisp while the center of it all remains tender, your savory smile. This guilty pleasure of mine.

A Distorted Image

The red bulb above my head allowed the perfect amount of light for me to see what I had to do. My job was simple. Inside the tiny dark room was enough space for one person to work. On the back wall was the supply cabinet, I never looked in there. The hum of the machine was my only company. Consistency was key, unclip the cartridge, slide the small film out of its case and feed it into the machine. No longer the dip and drip process, this automatic marvel would take a few minutes to produce a black and white image. The darkness made it possible. My fingers moved quickly, my attention drawn to heavy breathing behind me. I was not alone. The hot breath landed on the back of my neck, a low mumble alongside my ear, words I could not decipher. I was pinned against the counter. The weight of his body held me there. The tiny films dropped to the floor. I was as quiet as the room, my voice went missing. Uninvited hands on my body, I needed this to stop immediately like the red light above my head suggested. Exposing this person like the film on the floor was my best defense. I flipped the switch, no longer in the dark.

Aubade In The Afternoon

The quiet of winter escorts the sun. He encouraged her to declare herself. The light skates across the floor in figure eights. *I am a poet,* she spoke to the empty room. An orchid in rebloom pivots to capture the light when no one is looking.

Forty Weeks Times Six

Completely mine when your heartbeat inside of me. It was implied we would grow together. Measures were taken to remember. Photos, special songs, and cakes adorned with candles. Each of you bloomed, becoming exactly who you were supposed to be extraordinary, nothing I could ever imagine. I watched it all like a movie, your characters evolved. I cheered you all on, wiped your faces, and tried to keep my opinions to myself, the later being the most difficult. A privilege to mentor each of you, while joy and sadness filled the space we shared when you were completely mine.

Nameless Bakery

On the corner, from the apartment on Brady Street, was their place. The actual name, a few lost letters on the front window remain. When they first met, out of character, she asked him to sit down. He drank black coffee. She drank tea from a chipped cup with yellow roses (her favorite). She kept the apartment. He moved on. Some of the reasons lost like the lettering of the bakery. Still, she carries her sadness like a stack of overdue library books, drinks coffee now--black. The idea of him lingers like powdered sugar on the lips.

A Bit On The Side

Imported cheeses aged to perfection hung like golden lanterns suspended overhead. A ceramic gondola filled with salty olives, crusty bread, and hot peppers, a portal to his homeland. Dried meats, the connective tissue strung alongside the cheese draped the restaurant's ceiling, a marriage held together by its string, once as sweet as an anisette cookie. Family recipes proudly prepared and served up fresh daily. His family crest worn upon his apron, the secret ingredients his wife held the key. The gentleman, a new regular, sat solo at a table reserved for two. His appetite ravenous he devoured what was put in front of him each bite savored. The chefs' thoughts simmered, as he served the gentlemen's meal perfectly seasoned on a bitter plate of broccoli rabe. The gentleman desired the chef's secrets, a taste he wanted to make his own. He made his gratitude evident, the chef served him seconds.

Kaleidoscope Vision

Look, I had always been a tree hugger. My arms wrapped around the vastness of all your needs, my nails dug deep into your skin and yet I would bleed the color of your eyes. Dressed to please, my colorful arsenal camouflaged my existence allowing you the spotlight, basking in your glory, this chameleon learned how to adapt to be who you needed me to be. My stinky tongue spit out what was expected of me, as I stored my words in a vault. The right eye never lost sight of your next move as my left eye scanned the world. Thick skin protected my vulnerable self. I shed the hurt and saved the layers to warm my bed. When you gripped my neck I lost my balance and landed on my back, a tactic used to keep me under control. Careful not to twist myself in knots I slipped away like lizards do.

Borrowed And Blue

Never just about sex, our love held promise / It protected us / It held dreams / It made us laugh / It was playful / It was a commitment / It created a family / It carried hard times / It felt joyous / It lost the magic / It became angry / It lost tolerance / It misplaced respect / It got lonely / became just about sex.

Hothouse

Must Love Plants, Inquire Within: a rusty nail held the weight of the sign. The morning light danced upon the bromeliad blooming a soft hue, the fuzz on a summer's peach. I spied my reflection against glass panes highlighting the corners of my eyes. Thin lines like vines cascade downward land upon my lips, a dusty rose. In a moment of urgency, I grab the sign off the nail and step inside. A foundation dug by hand, soil settled under my fingernails. A worn denim apron and an orchid kiss smudge my nametag. My calloused hands grasp terracotta pots, hold space for untouched dreams. A Tuscan sunset. The conservatory protects from harsh elements. The sanctuary quiets my mind. This part-time job. Growth surrounds me as I water and prune, while spiders trapeze above my head.

Pillow Talk

What if I could
call you my lover
feel the weight of your troubles
between torn sheets

I would sweep away
your heartache
while dust bunnies dance
under our bed

What if life offered
second chances
and time stood down

Sunbeams curtsied
at the sound of your laugh

I would lasso George Bailey's
moon and use it
as a headlamp
Shine light on what's hidden

What if I couldn't find you
and the world grew dark
shadows crying in despair

I would whisper your name
into my pillow
while cold sheets
replaced your touch

The Phone Never Rang This Morning

Eight O'five / Your voice suspended in my head like the embroidered handkerchief held by a thread. Each year your call marked my trip around the sun. *This is the exact time you were born, Cheryl Ann.* I failed to recognize the weight in the gesture until now. This morning / the phone like a broken clock. Eight O'six.

Roadside Memorial, Route 80, (To Michigan)

Billboards, road signs, countless water bottles,
the lonely shoe.

Radio set at 106.7—vocals, karaoke-style. No microphone necessary. I cruise along at 58 mph, dusty sunbeams reflect on my sunglasses (rims Elton John would approve).

White crosses, so many crosses. Angels and angels and angels. Weather-beaten memorials: deflated balloons, faded stuffed animals, plastic flowers that will never perish. Names inscribed, rainbow colors pay homage. Markers positioned where loved ones died.

Life ends without permission, moves forward the same way.

Homestead Farm At Oak Ridge

The portal to the place adults weren't allowed and we made up the rules. Got a running start, grabbed the rope, and flew across the water where turtles lived in walls of mud and golf balls gathered. *Pumpkin Patch Creek,* the nemesis of every golfer on the thirteenth hole of the Oakridge Golf Course. A creek that swallowed the promises of misbegotten golfers. Harry would wade in the creek and collect the errant shots, and it was my job to wash them to make them shiny. It was a small enterprise with no overhead and the hours were flexible. Ten cents a ball was the going rate. If you paid a dollar you got a baker's dozen. Neatly stored in cardboard egg cartons made the presentation attractive, sales were good. The golf course shut down, my brother is gone, yellow flowers still bloom on the bank of that creek.

Effervescent Memories
For Lorenzo (Larry) Peluso

We drank a toast to innocence we drank a toast to time reliving, in our eloquence another "Auld Lang Syne."
   -Dan Fogelberg, song lyric from
   "Same Auld Lang Syne" 1981

Champagne could be ginger ale in a child's hands. *Come on Cheryl, they'll never notice.* My cousin's request; eldest grandchild, I held the authority to shut down the champagne switch. New Year's Eve, Shirley Temple drinks, maraschino cherries — now scarlet lipstick, a midnight kiss. Prisms circulate overhead, a crystal ball countdown. Dick Clark chants 10... 9... 8... raise your fluted glass. The sip tickles my nose. 7...6...5... laughter fills the room. 4...3...2... tears flow. 1... *Happy New Year!* Hugs and kisses all around. My final hug always reserved for grandpa.

Abundance

She dug deep, unearthed hidden bounty, shrouded in darkness, a potatoes eye grasping for light. Unleashed her portal outward, she sang a cardinals sonnet. Desire no longer taboo, her thirst for life's challenges blossomed. Cultivated harvest, a plentiful cornucopia.

Moving On

Her words still linger like a gardenia bloom.

Use the fancy teacup everyday Cheryl Ann, you can't take it with you.

When I die I am taking everything with me.
Box the rest and give it away.

I am taking my voice.
The assertive tone, my desire to be heard.

The smile, with the tiny chipped tooth that complimented the scar above my left eye, the visual reminder of painful times.

My eyes that witnessed such beauty, closed when I kissed soft lips.
I'll take my lips too!

The freckles come with me, sunkissed blemishes that held secrets.

My uterus may as well tag along, after all its worn out,
It would be useless to anyone else.

My sense of humor is up for grabs.

My love of travel will move on with me, there will be no need for luggage.

I will take my good intentions, they won't matter any longer.

My fears and grief will leave with me.
Powerless once and for all.

And what of the literal heart? Is that where the love for my children, music and dance lived? I'll keep them.

The rest goes!

Please donate my fancy tea cup to the local thrift shop.

NOTES & ACKNOWLEDGMENTS

Thank you to the editors of the following journals in which these poems first appeared, many in earlier versions:

Exit 13 Magazine: "The Ladies of Schwin Drive"
Exit 13 Magazine: "Song Sung Blue, Overlook Hospital
               Summit, New Jersey"
Ponder Savant: "Solitude"
Lion and Lilac Arts: "Off My Mark"
Lion and Lilac Arts: "Flecks of Light"
The Raconteur Review: "Nameless Bakery"
Tiferet: "Roadside Memorials, Route 80, (To Michigan)"
Written Tales: "Effervescent Memories"
Big Hammer: "Kaleidoscope Vision"
Big Hammer: "A Distorted Image"
Ovunque Siamo: "A Bit On The Side"

I would like to thank my publisher, Dave Roskos, for believing in this book.

Made in the USA
Middletown, DE
07 August 2024